# This
# Drone Flight Log Book
## Belongs to

_____

_____

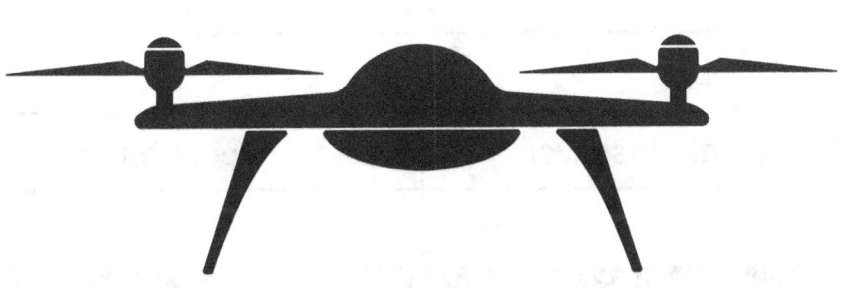

# Drone Flight Log Book

Date:

## Drone Model Name

| Location (from-to) | Time |
|---|---|
|  |  |

| Minutes of flight | Battery |
|---|---|
|  |  |

| Weather | Temperature | Wind speed | Wind Direction |
|---|---|---|---|
|  |  |  |  |

| Crew ||
|---|---|
| Visual Observer | Operator |
|  |  |

| Flight Mission | Notes |
|---|---|

# Drone Flight Log Book

Date:

## Drone Model Name

| Location (from - to) | Time |
|---|---|
|  |  |
| Minutes of flight | Battery |
|  |  |

| Weather | Temperature | Wind speed | Wind Direction |
|---|---|---|---|
|  |  |  |  |

| Crew ||
|---|---|
| Visiual Observer | Operator |
|  |  |

| Flight Mission | Notes |
|---|---|
|  |  |

# Drone Flight Log Book

Date:

## Drone Model Name

| Location (from-to) | Time |
|---|---|
|  |  |
| Minutes of flight | Battery |
|  |  |

| Weather | Temperature | Wind speed | Wind Direction |
|---|---|---|---|
|  |  |  |  |

| Crew ||
|---|---|
| Visual Observer | Operator |
|  |  |

| Flight Mission | Notes |
|---|---|
|  |  |

# Drone Flight Log Book

Date:

## Drone Model Name

| Location (from - to) | Time |
|---|---|
| | |

| Minutes of flight | Battery |
|---|---|
| | |

| Weather | Temperature | Wind speed | Wind Direction |
|---|---|---|---|
| | | | |

| Crew ||
|---|---|
| Visiual Observer | Operator |
| | |
| Flight Mission | Notes |

# Drone Flight Log Book

Date:

## Drone Model Name

| Location (from-to) | Time |
|---|---|
|  |  |
| Minutes of flight | Battery |
|  |  |

| Weather | Temperature | Wind speed | Wind Direction |
|---|---|---|---|
|  |  |  |  |

| Crew ||
|---|---|
| Visual Observer | Operator |
|  |  |

| Flight Mission | Notes |
|---|---|
|  |  |

# Drone Flight Log Book

Date:

## Drone Model Name

| Location (from - to) | Time |
|---|---|
|  |  |
| Minutes of flight | Battery |
|  |  |

| Weather | Temperature | Wind speed | Wind Direction |
|---|---|---|---|
|  |  |  |  |

| Crew ||
|---|---|
| Visiual Observer | Operator |
|  |  |

| Flight Mission | Notes |
|---|---|
|  |  |

# Drone Flight Log Book

Date:

## Drone Model Name

| Location (from-to) | Time |
|---|---|
|  |  |

| Minutes of flight | Battery |
|---|---|
|  |  |

| Weather | Temperature | Wind speed | Wind Direction |
|---|---|---|---|
|  |  |  |  |

| Crew ||
|---|---|
| Visual Observer | Operator |
|  |  |

| Flight Mission | Notes |
|---|---|
|  |  |

# Drone Flight Log Book

Date:

## Drone Model Name

| Location (from - to) | Time |
|---|---|
|  |  |
| Minutes of flight | Battery |
|  |  |

| Weather | Temperature | Wind speed | Wind Direction |
|---|---|---|---|
|  |  |  |  |

| Crew ||
|---|---|
| Visiual Observer | Operator |
|  |  |
| Flight Mission | Notes |

# Drone Flight Log Book

Date:

## Drone Model Name

| Location (from-to) | Time |
|---|---|
|  |  |
| Minutes of flight | Battery |
|  |  |

| Weather | Temperature | Wind speed | Wind Direction |
|---|---|---|---|
|  |  |  |  |

| Crew ||
|---|---|
| Visual Observer | Operator |
|  |  |
| **Flight Mission** | **Notes** |

# Drone Flight Log Book

Date:

## Drone Model Name

| Location (from - to) | Time |
|---|---|
|  |  |
| Minutes of flight | Battery |
|  |  |

| Weather | Temperature | Wind speed | Wind Direction |
|---|---|---|---|
|  |  |  |  |

| Crew ||
|---|---|
| Visiual Observer | Operator |
|  |  |
| Flight Mission | Notes |

# Drone Flight Log Book

Date:

## Drone Model Name

| Location (from-to) | Time |
|---|---|
|  |  |
| Minutes of flight | Battery |
|  |  |

| Weather | Temperature | Wind speed | Wind Direction |
|---|---|---|---|
|  |  |  |  |

| Crew ||
|---|---|
| Visual Observer | Operator |
|  |  |

**Flight Mission** — **Notes**

# Drone Flight Log Book

Date:

## Drone Model Name

| Location (from - to) | Time |
|---|---|
|  |  |

| Minutes of flight | Battery |
|---|---|
|  |  |

| Weather | Temperature | Wind speed | Wind Direction |
|---|---|---|---|
|  |  |  |  |

| Crew ||
|---|---|
| Visiual Observer | Operator |
|  |  |

| Flight Mission | Notes |
|---|---|
|  |  |

# Drone Flight Log Book

Date:

## Drone Model Name

| Location (from-to) | Time |
|---|---|
|  |  |
| Minutes of flight | Battery |
|  |  |

| Weather | Temperature | Wind speed | Wind Direction |
|---|---|---|---|
|  |  |  |  |

| Crew ||
|---|---|
| Visual Observer | Operator |
|  |  |

**Flight Mission** — **Notes**

# Drone Flight Log Book

Date:

## Drone Model Name

| Location (from - to) | Time |
|---|---|
|  |  |

| Minutes of flight | Battery |
|---|---|
|  |  |

| Weather | Temperature | Wind speed | Wind Direction |
|---|---|---|---|
|  |  |  |  |

| Crew ||
|---|---|
| Visiual Observer | Operator |
|  |  |

| Flight Mission | Notes |
|---|---|
|  |  |

# Drone Flight Log Book

Date:

Drone Model Name

| Location (from-to) | Time |
|---|---|
|  |  |
| Minutes of flight | Battery |
|  |  |

| Weather | Temperature | Wind speed | Wind Direction |
|---|---|---|---|
|  |  |  |  |

| Crew ||
|---|---|
| Visual Observer | Operator |
|  |  |

Flight Mission | Notes

# Drone Flight Log Book

Date:

## Drone Model Name

| Location (from - to) | Time |
|---|---|
|  |  |
| Minutes of flight | Battery |
|  |  |

| Weather | Temperature | Wind speed | Wind Direction |
|---|---|---|---|
|  |  |  |  |

| Crew ||
|---|---|
| Visiual Observer | Operator |
|  |  |

| Flight Mission | Notes |
|---|---|

# Drone Flight Log Book

Date:

## Drone Model Name

| Location (from-to) | Time |
|---|---|
|  |  |
| Minutes of flight | Battery |
|  |  |

| Weather | Temperature | Wind speed | Wind Direction |
|---|---|---|---|
|  |  |  |  |

| Crew ||
|---|---|
| Visual Observer | Operator |
|  |  |
| **Flight Mission** | **Notes** |

# Drone Flight Log Book

Date:

## Drone Model Name

| Location (from - to) | Time |
|---|---|
|  |  |
| Minutes of flight | Battery |
|  |  |

| Weather | Temperature | Wind speed | Wind Direction |
|---|---|---|---|
|  |  |  |  |

| Crew ||
|---|---|
| Visiual Observer | Operator |
|  |  |

| Flight Mission | Notes |
|---|---|

# Drone Flight Log Book

Date:

Drone Model Name

| Location (from-to) | Time |
|---|---|
|  |  |

| Minutes of flight | Battery |
|---|---|
|  |  |

| Weather | Temperature | Wind speed | Wind Direction |
|---|---|---|---|
|  |  |  |  |

| Crew ||
|---|---|
| Visual Observer | Operator |
|  |  |

| Flight Mission | Notes |
|---|---|

# Drone Flight Log Book

Date:

## Drone Model Name

| Location (from - to) | Time |
|---|---|
| | |

| Minutes of flight | Battery |
|---|---|
| | |

| Weather | Temperature | Wind speed | Wind Direction |
|---|---|---|---|
| | | | |

| Crew ||
|---|---|
| Visiual Observer | Operator |
| | |
| Flight Mission | Notes |

# Drone Flight Log Book

Date:

## Drone Model Name

| Location (from-to) | Time |
|---|---|
|  |  |
| Minutes of flight | Battery |
|  |  |

| Weather | Temperature | Wind speed | Wind Direction |
|---|---|---|---|
|  |  |  |  |

| Crew ||
|---|---|
| Visual Observer | Operator |
|  |  |
| **Flight Mission** | **Notes** |

# Drone Flight Log Book

Date:

## Drone Model Name

| Location (from - to) | Time |
|---|---|
|  |  |
| Minutes of flight | Battery |
|  |  |

| Weather | Temperature | Wind speed | Wind Direction |
|---|---|---|---|
|  |  |  |  |

| Crew ||
|---|---|
| Visiual Observer | Operator |
|  |  |
| Flight Mission | Notes |

# Drone Flight Log Book

Date:

## Drone Model Name

| Location (from-to) | Time |
|---|---|
|  |  |
| Minutes of flight | Battery |
|  |  |

| Weather | Temperature | Wind speed | Wind Direction |
|---|---|---|---|
|  |  |  |  |

| Crew ||
|---|---|
| Visual Observer | Operator |
|  |  |
| Flight Mission | Notes |

# Drone Flight Log Book

Date:

## Drone Model Name

| Location (from - to) | Time |
|---|---|
|  |  |
| Minutes of flight | Battery |
|  |  |

| Weather | Temperature | Wind speed | Wind Direction |
|---|---|---|---|
|  |  |  |  |

| Crew ||
|---|---|
| Visiual Observer | Operator |
|  |  |
| Flight Mission | Notes |

# Drone Flight Log Book

Date:

## Drone Model Name

| Location (from-to) | Time |
|---|---|
|  |  |
| Minutes of flight | Battery |
|  |  |

| Weather | Temperature | Wind speed | Wind Direction |
|---|---|---|---|
|  |  |  |  |

| Crew ||
|---|---|
| Visual Observer | Operator |
|  |  |
| **Flight Mission** | **Notes** |

# Drone Flight Log Book

Date:

## Drone Model Name

| Location (from - to) | Time |
|---|---|
|  |  |

| Minutes of flight | Battery |
|---|---|
|  |  |

| Weather | Temperature | Wind speed | Wind Direction |
|---|---|---|---|
|  |  |  |  |

| Crew ||
|---|---|
| Visiual Observer | Operator |
|  |  |

| Flight Mission | Notes |
|---|---|
|  |  |

# Drone Flight Log Book

Date:

## Drone Model Name

| Location (from-to) | Time |
|---|---|
|  |  |
| Minutes of flight | Battery |
|  |  |

| Weather | Temperature | Wind speed | Wind Direction |
|---|---|---|---|
|  |  |  |  |

| Crew ||
|---|---|
| Visual Observer | Operator |
|  |  |

| Flight Mission | Notes |
|---|---|

# Drone Flight Log Book

Date:

## Drone Model Name

| Location (from - to) | Time |
|---|---|
|  |  |

| Minutes of flight | Battery |
|---|---|
|  |  |

| Weather | Temperature | Wind speed | Wind Direction |
|---|---|---|---|
|  |  |  |  |

| Crew ||
|---|---|
| Visiual Observer | Operator |
|  |  |

| Flight Mission | Notes |
|---|---|

# Drone Flight Log Book

Date:

## Drone Model Name

| Location (from-to) | Time |
|---|---|
|  |  |
| Minutes of flight | Battery |
|  |  |

| Weather | Temperature | Wind speed | Wind Direction |
|---|---|---|---|
|  |  |  |  |

| Crew ||
|---|---|
| Visual Observer | Operator |
|  |  |
| Flight Mission | Notes |
|  |  |

# Drone Flight Log Book

Date:

## Drone Model Name

| Location (from - to) | Time |
|---|---|
|  |  |

| Minutes of flight | Battery |
|---|---|
|  |  |

| Weather | Temperature | Wind speed | Wind Direction |
|---|---|---|---|
|  |  |  |  |

| Crew ||
|---|---|
| Visiual Observer | Operator |
|  |  |

| Flight Mission | Notes |
|---|---|
|  |  |

# Drone Flight Log Book

Date:

## Drone Model Name

| Location (from-to) | Time |
|---|---|
|  |  |

| Minutes of flight | Battery |
|---|---|
|  |  |

| Weather | Temperature | Wind speed | Wind Direction |
|---|---|---|---|
|  |  |  |  |

| Crew ||
|---|---|
| Visual Observer | Operator |
|  |  |

| Flight Mission | Notes |

# Drone Flight Log Book

Date:

## Drone Model Name

| Location (from - to) | Time |
|---|---|
|  |  |
| Minutes of flight | Battery |
|  |  |

| Weather | Temperature | Wind speed | Wind Direction |
|---|---|---|---|
|  |  |  |  |

| Crew ||
|---|---|
| Visiual Observer | Operator |
|  |  |

**Flight Mission** — **Notes**

# Drone Flight Log Book

Date:

## Drone Model Name

| Location (from-to) | Time |
|---|---|
|  |  |
| Minutes of flight | Battery |
|  |  |

| Weather | Temperature | Wind speed | Wind Direction |
|---|---|---|---|
|  |  |  |  |

| Crew ||
|---|---|
| Visual Observer | Operator |
|  |  |
| Flight Mission | Notes |

# Drone Flight Log Book

Date:

## Drone Model Name

| Location (from - to) | Time |
|---|---|
|  |  |
| Minutes of flight | Battery |
|  |  |

| Weather | Temperature | Wind speed | Wind Direction |
|---|---|---|---|
|  |  |  |  |

| Crew ||
|---|---|
| Visiual Observer | Operator |
|  |  |
| Flight Mission | Notes |

# Drone Flight Log Book

Date:

## Drone Model Name

| Location (from-to) | Time |
|---|---|
|  |  |
| Minutes of flight | Battery |
|  |  |

| Weather | Temperature | Wind speed | Wind Direction |
|---|---|---|---|
|  |  |  |  |

| Crew ||
|---|---|
| Visual Observer | Operator |
|  |  |

| Flight Mission | Notes |
|---|---|

# Drone Flight Log Book

Date:

## Drone Model Name

| Location (from - to) | Time |
|---|---|
|  |  |
| Minutes of flight | Battery |
|  |  |

| Weather | Temperature | Wind speed | Wind Direction |
|---|---|---|---|
|  |  |  |  |

| Crew ||
|---|---|
| Visiual Observer | Operator |
|  |  |

| Flight Mission | Notes |
|---|---|

# Drone Flight Log Book

Date:

## Drone Model Name

| Location (from-to) | Time |
|---|---|
|  |  |

| Minutes of flight | Battery |
|---|---|
|  |  |

| Weather | Temperature | Wind speed | Wind Direction |
|---|---|---|---|
|  |  |  |  |

| Crew ||
|---|---|
| Visual Observer | Operator |
|  |  |

**Flight Mission** — **Notes**

# Drone Flight Log Book

Date:

## Drone Model Name

| Location (from - to) | Time |
|---|---|
|  |  |//
| Minutes of flight | Battery |
|  |  |

| Weather | Temperature | Wind speed | Wind Direction |
|---|---|---|---|
|  |  |  |  |

| Crew ||
|---|---|
| Visiual Observer | Operator |
|  |  |

| Flight Mission | Notes |
|---|---|
|  |  |

# Drone Flight Log Book

Date:

## Drone Model Name

| Location (from-to) | Time |
|---|---|
|  |  |
| Minutes of flight | Battery |
|  |  |

| Weather | Temperature | Wind speed | Wind Direction |
|---|---|---|---|
|  |  |  |  |

| Crew ||
|---|---|
| Visual Observer | Operator |
|  |  |

| Flight Mission | Notes |
|---|---|

# Drone Flight Log Book

Date:

## Drone Model Name

| Location (from - to) | Time |
|---|---|
|  |  |

| Minutes of flight | Battery |
|---|---|
|  |  |

| Weather | Temperature | Wind speed | Wind Direction |
|---|---|---|---|
|  |  |  |  |

| Crew ||
|---|---|
| Visiual Observer | Operator |
|  |  |

| Flight Mission | Notes |
|---|---|
|  |  |

# Drone Flight Log Book

Date:

## Drone Model Name

| Location (from-to) | Time |
|---|---|
|  |  |
| Minutes of flight | Battery |
|  |  |

| Weather | Temperature | Wind speed | Wind Direction |
|---|---|---|---|
|  |  |  |  |

| Crew ||
|---|---|
| Visual Observer | Operator |
|  |  |
| Flight Mission | Notes |

# Drone Flight Log Book

Date:

## Drone Model Name

| Location (from - to) | Time |
|---|---|
|  |  |
| Minutes of flight | Battery |
|  |  |

| Weather | Temperature | Wind speed | Wind Direction |
|---|---|---|---|
|  |  |  |  |

| Crew ||
|---|---|
| Visiual Observer | Operator |
|  |  |
| Flight Mission | Notes |

# Drone Flight Log Book

Date:

## Drone Model Name

| Location (from-to) | Time |
|---|---|
|  |  |
| Minutes of flight | Battery |
|  |  |

| Weather | Temperature | Wind speed | Wind Direction |
|---|---|---|---|
|  |  |  |  |

| Crew ||
|---|---|
| Visual Observer | Operator |
|  |  |
| Flight Mission | Notes |

# Drone Flight Log Book

Date:

## Drone Model Name

| Location (from - to) | Time |
|---|---|
|  |  |
| Minutes of flight | Battery |
|  |  |

| Weather | Temperature | Wind speed | Wind Direction |
|---|---|---|---|
|  |  |  |  |

| Crew ||
|---|---|
| Visiual Observer | Operator |
|  |  |

| Flight Mission | Notes |
|---|---|
|  |  |

# Drone Flight Log Book

Date:

## Drone Model Name

| Location (from-to) | Time |
|---|---|
|  |  |
| Minutes of flight | Battery |
|  |  |

| Weather | Temperature | Wind speed | Wind Direction |
|---|---|---|---|
|  |  |  |  |

| Crew ||
|---|---|
| Visual Observer | Operator |
|  |  |
| **Flight Mission** | **Notes** |

# Drone Flight Log Book

Date:

Drone Model Name

| Location (from - to) | Time |
|---|---|
|  |  |
| Minutes of flight | Battery |
|  |  |

| Weather | Temperature | Wind speed | Wind Direction |
|---|---|---|---|
|  |  |  |  |

| Crew ||
|---|---|
| Visiual Observer | Operator |
|  |  |
| Flight Mission | Notes |

# Drone Flight Log Book

Date:

## Drone Model Name

| Location (from-to) | Time |
|---|---|
|  |  |
| Minutes of flight | Battery |
|  |  |

| Weather | Temperature | Wind speed | Wind Direction |
|---|---|---|---|
|  |  |  |  |

| Crew ||
|---|---|
| Visual Observer | Operator |
|  |  |// 

| Flight Mission | Notes |
|---|---|
|  |  |

# Drone Flight Log Book

Date:

## Drone Model Name

| Location (from - to) | Time |
|---|---|
|  |  |
| Minutes of flight | Battery |
|  |  |

| Weather | Temperature | Wind speed | Wind Direction |
|---|---|---|---|
|  |  |  |  |

| Crew ||
|---|---|
| Visiual Observer | Operator |
|  |  |
| Flight Mission | Notes |

# Drone Flight Log Book

Date:

## Drone Model Name

| Location (from-to) | Time |
|---|---|
|  |  |
| Minutes of flight | Battery |
|  |  |

| Weather | Temperature | Wind speed | Wind Direction |
|---|---|---|---|
|  |  |  |  |

| Crew ||
|---|---|
| Visual Observer | Operator |
|  |  |

**Flight Mission** | **Notes**

# Drone Flight Log Book

Date:

## Drone Model Name

| Location (from - to) | Time |
|---|---|
|  |  |
| Minutes of flight | Battery |
|  |  |

| Weather | Temperature | Wind speed | Wind Direction |
|---|---|---|---|
|  |  |  |  |

| Crew ||
|---|---|
| Visiual Observer | Operator |
|  |  |
| Flight Mission | Notes |

# Drone Flight Log Book

Date:

## Drone Model Name

| Location (from-to) | Time |
|---|---|
|  |  |
| Minutes of flight | Battery |
|  |  |

| Weather | Temperature | Wind speed | Wind Direction |
|---|---|---|---|
|  |  |  |  |

### Crew

| Visual Observer | Operator |
|---|---|
|  |  |

| Flight Mission | Notes |
|---|---|

# Drone Flight Log Book

Date:

## Drone Model Name

| Location (from - to) | Time |
|---|---|
|  |  |
| Minutes of flight | Battery |
|  |  |

| Weather | Temperature | Wind speed | Wind Direction |
|---|---|---|---|
|  |  |  |  |

| Crew ||
|---|---|
| Visiual Observer | Operator |
|  |  |
| Flight Mission | Notes |

# Drone Flight Log Book

Date:

Drone Model Name

| Location (from-to) | Time |
|---|---|
|  |  |
| Minutes of flight | Battery |
|  |  |

| Weather | Temperature | Wind speed | Wind Direction |
|---|---|---|---|
|  |  |  |  |

| Crew ||
|---|---|
| Visual Observer | Operator |
|  |  |
| Flight Mission | Notes |

# Drone Flight Log Book

Date:

## Drone Model Name

| Location (from - to) | Time |
|---|---|
|  |  |

| Minutes of flight | Battery |
|---|---|
|  |  |

| Weather | Temperature | Wind speed | Wind Direction |
|---|---|---|---|
|  |  |  |  |

| Crew ||
|---|---|
| Visiual Observer | Operator |
|  |  |

| Flight Mission | Notes |
|---|---|
|  |  |

# Drone Flight Log Book

Date:

## Drone Model Name

| Location (from-to) | Time |
|---|---|
|  |  |
| **Minutes of flight** | **Battery** |
|  |  |

| Weather | Temperature | Wind speed | Wind Direction |
|---|---|---|---|
|  |  |  |  |

| Crew ||
|---|---|
| Visual Observer | Operator |
|  |  |
| **Flight Mission** | **Notes** |
|  |  |

# Drone Flight Log Book

Date:

## Drone Model Name

| Location (from - to) | Time |
|---|---|
|  |  |
| Minutes of flight | Battery |
|  |  |

| Weather | Temperature | Wind speed | Wind Direction |
|---|---|---|---|
|  |  |  |  |

| Crew ||
|---|---|
| Visiual Observer | Operator |
|  |  |
| Flight Mission | Notes |

# Drone Flight Log Book

Date:

Drone Model Name

| Location (from-to) | Time |
|---|---|
|  |  |
| Minutes of flight | Battery |
|  |  |

| Weather | Temperature | Wind speed | Wind Direction |
|---|---|---|---|
|  |  |  |  |

| Crew ||
|---|---|
| Visual Observer | Operator |
|  |  |

| Flight Mission | Notes |
|---|---|

# Drone Flight Log Book

Date:

## Drone Model Name

| Location (from - to) | Time |
|---|---|
|  |  |
| **Minutes of flight** | **Battery** |
|  |  |

| Weather | Temperature | Wind speed | Wind Direction |
|---|---|---|---|
|  |  |  |  |

| Crew ||
|---|---|
| Visiual Observer | Operator |
|  |  |
| **Flight Mission** | **Notes** |

# Drone Flight Log Book

Date:

## Drone Model Name

| Location (from-to) | Time |
|---|---|
| | |
| Minutes of flight | Battery |
| | |

| Weather | Temperature | Wind speed | Wind Direction |
|---|---|---|---|
| | | | |

| Crew ||
|---|---|
| Visual Observer | Operator |
| | |//
| Flight Mission | Notes |
| | |

# Drone Flight Log Book

Date:

## Drone Model Name

| Location (from - to) | Time |
|---|---|
|  |  |
| Minutes of flight | Battery |
|  |  |

| Weather | Temperature | Wind speed | Wind Direction |
|---|---|---|---|
|  |  |  |  |

| Crew ||
|---|---|
| Visiual Observer | Operator |
|  |  |
| Flight Mission | Notes |
|  |  |

# Drone Flight Log Book

Date:

## Drone Model Name

| Location (from-to) | Time |
|---|---|
|  |  |
| Minutes of flight | Battery |
|  |  |

| Weather | Temperature | Wind speed | Wind Direction |
|---|---|---|---|
|  |  |  |  |

| Crew ||
|---|---|
| Visual Observer | Operator |
|  |  |
| Flight Mission | Notes |

# Drone Flight Log Book

Date:

## Drone Model Name

| Location (from - to) | Time |
|---|---|
|  |  |
| Minutes of flight | Battery |
|  |  |

| Weather | Temperature | Wind speed | Wind Direction |
|---|---|---|---|
|  |  |  |  |

| Crew ||
|---|---|
| Visiual Observer | Operator |
|  |  |
| **Flight Mission** | **Notes** |

# Drone Flight Log Book

Date:

## Drone Model Name

| Location (from-to) | Time |
|---|---|
|  |  |
| Minutes of flight | Battery |
|  |  |

| Weather | Temperature | Wind speed | Wind Direction |
|---|---|---|---|
|  |  |  |  |

| Crew ||
|---|---|
| Visual Observer | Operator |
|  |  |

| Flight Mission | Notes |
|---|---|
|  |  |

# Drone Flight Log Book

Date:

## Drone Model Name

| Location (from - to) | Time |
|---|---|
|  |  |
| Minutes of flight | Battery |
|  |  |

| Weather | Temperature | Wind speed | Wind Direction |
|---|---|---|---|
|  |  |  |  |

| Crew ||
|---|---|
| Visiual Observer | Operator |
|  |  |
| Flight Mission | Notes |

# Drone Flight Log Book

Date:

## Drone Model Name

| Location (from-to) | Time |
|---|---|
|  |  |
| Minutes of flight | Battery |
|  |  |

| Weather | Temperature | Wind speed | Wind Direction |
|---|---|---|---|
|  |  |  |  |

| Crew ||
|---|---|
| Visual Observer | Operator |
|  |  |

| Flight Mission | Notes |
|---|---|
|  |  |

# Drone Flight Log Book

Date:

## Drone Model Name

| Location (from - to) | Time |
|---|---|
|  |  |
| Minutes of flight | Battery |
|  |  |

| Weather | Temperature | Wind speed | Wind Direction |
|---|---|---|---|
|  |  |  |  |

| Crew ||
|---|---|
| Visiual Observer | Operator |
|  |  |
| Flight Mission | Notes |

# Drone Flight Log Book

Date:

## Drone Model Name

| Location (from-to) | Time |
|---|---|
|  |  |
| Minutes of flight | Battery |
|  |  |

| Weather | Temperature | Wind speed | Wind Direction |
|---|---|---|---|
|  |  |  |  |

### Crew

| Visual Observer | Operator |
|---|---|
|  |  |

Flight Mission | Notes

# Drone Flight Log Book

Date:

## Drone Model Name

| Location (from - to) | Time |
|---|---|
|  |  |
| Minutes of flight | Battery |
|  |  |

| Weather | Temperature | Wind speed | Wind Direction |
|---|---|---|---|
|  |  |  |  |

| Crew ||
|---|---|
| Visiual Observer | Operator |
|  |  |

| Flight Mission | Notes |
|---|---|
|  |  |

# Drone Flight Log Book

Date:

## Drone Model Name

| Location (from-to) | Time |
|---|---|
|  |  |
| Minutes of flight | Battery |
|  |  |

| Weather | Temperature | Wind speed | Wind Direction |
|---|---|---|---|
|  |  |  |  |

| Crew ||
|---|---|
| Visual Observer | Operator |
|  |  |

| Flight Mission | Notes |
|---|---|
|  |  |

# Drone Flight Log Book

Date:

## Drone Model Name

| Location (from - to) | Time |
|---|---|
|  |  |

| Minutes of flight | Battery |
|---|---|
|  |  |

| Weather | Temperature | Wind speed | Wind Direction |
|---|---|---|---|
|  |  |  |  |

| Crew ||
|---|---|
| Visiual Observer | Operator |
|  |  |

| Flight Mission | Notes |
|---|---|

# Drone Flight Log Book

Date:

Drone Model Name

| Location (from-to) | Time |
|---|---|
|  |  |
| Minutes of flight | Battery |
|  |  |

| Weather | Temperature | Wind speed | Wind Direction |
|---|---|---|---|
|  |  |  |  |

| Crew ||
|---|---|
| Visual Observer | Operator |
|  |  |

| Flight Mission | Notes |
|---|---|
|  |  |

# Drone Flight Log Book

Date:

## Drone Model Name

| Location (from - to) | Time |
|---|---|
|  |  |
| Minutes of flight | Battery |
|  |  |

| Weather | Temperature | Wind speed | Wind Direction |
|---|---|---|---|
|  |  |  |  |

| Crew ||
|---|---|
| Visiual Observer | Operator |
|  |  |
| Flight Mission | Notes |

# Drone Flight Log Book

Date:

## Drone Model Name

| Location (from-to) | Time |
|---|---|
|  |  |
| Minutes of flight | Battery |
|  |  |

| Weather | Temperature | Wind speed | Wind Direction |
|---|---|---|---|
|  |  |  |  |

| Crew ||
|---|---|
| Visual Observer | Operator |
|  |  |
| Flight Mission | Notes |

# Drone Flight Log Book

Date:

## Drone Model Name

| Location (from - to) | Time |
|---|---|
|  |  |

| Minutes of flight | Battery |
|---|---|
|  |  |

| Weather | Temperature | Wind speed | Wind Direction |
|---|---|---|---|
|  |  |  |  |

| Crew ||
|---|---|
| Visiual Observer | Operator |
|  |  |

| Flight Mission | Notes |
|---|---|

# Drone Flight Log Book

Date:

Drone Model Name

| Location (from-to) | Time |
|---|---|
|  |  |
| Minutes of flight | Battery |
|  |  |

| Weather | Temperature | Wind speed | Wind Direction |
|---|---|---|---|
|  |  |  |  |

| Crew ||
|---|---|
| Visual Observer | Operator |
|  |  |
| Flight Mission | Notes |

# Drone Flight Log Book

Date:

## Drone Model Name

| Location (from - to) | Time |
|---|---|
|  |  |
| Minutes of flight | Battery |
|  |  |

| Weather | Temperature | Wind speed | Wind Direction |
|---|---|---|---|
|  |  |  |  |

| Crew ||
|---|---|
| Visiual Observer | Operator |
|  |  |
| **Flight Mission** | **Notes** |
|  |  |

# Drone Flight Log Book

Date:

## Drone Model Name

| Location (from-to) | Time |
|---|---|
|  |  |
| Minutes of flight | Battery |
|  |  |

| Weather | Temperature | Wind speed | Wind Direction |
|---|---|---|---|
|  |  |  |  |

| Crew ||
|---|---|
| Visual Observer | Operator |
|  |  |

| Flight Mission | Notes |
|---|---|
|  |  |

# Drone Flight Log Book

Date:

## Drone Model Name

| Location (from - to) | Time |
|---|---|
|  |  |
| Minutes of flight | Battery |
|  |  |

| Weather | Temperature | Wind speed | Wind Direction |
|---|---|---|---|
|  |  |  |  |

| Crew ||
|---|---|
| Visiual Observer | Operator |
|  |  |
| **Flight Mission** | **Notes** |

# Drone Flight Log Book

Date:

## Drone Model Name

| Location (from-to) | Time |
|---|---|
|  |  |
| Minutes of flight | Battery |
|  |  |

| Weather | Temperature | Wind speed | Wind Direction |
|---|---|---|---|
|  |  |  |  |

| Crew ||
|---|---|
| Visual Observer | Operator |
|  |  |
| Flight Mission | Notes |

# Drone Flight Log Book

Date:

Drone Model Name

| Location (from - to) | Time |
|---|---|
|  |  |

| Minutes of flight | Battery |
|---|---|
|  |  |

| Weather | Temperature | Wind speed | Wind Direction |
|---|---|---|---|
|  |  |  |  |

| Crew ||
|---|---|
| Visiual Observer | Operator |
|  |  |

| Flight Mission | Notes |
|---|---|

# Drone Flight Log Book

Date:

## Drone Model Name

| Location (from-to) | Time |
|---|---|
|  |  |

| Minutes of flight | Battery |
|---|---|
|  |  |

| Weather | Temperature | Wind speed | Wind Direction |
|---|---|---|---|
|  |  |  |  |

| Crew ||
|---|---|
| Visual Observer | Operator |
|  |  |

| Flight Mission | Notes |
|---|---|
|  |  |

# Drone Flight Log Book

Date:

## Drone Model Name

| Location (from - to) | Time |
|---|---|
|  |  |

| Minutes of flight | Battery |
|---|---|
|  |  |

| Weather | Temperature | Wind speed | Wind Direction |
|---|---|---|---|
|  |  |  |  |

| Crew ||
|---|---|
| Visiual Observer | Operator |
|  |  |

| Flight Mission | Notes |
|---|---|
|  |  |

# Drone Flight Log Book

Date:

## Drone Model Name

| Location (from-to) | Time |
|---|---|
|  |  |
| Minutes of flight | Battery |
|  |  |

| Weather | Temperature | Wind speed | Wind Direction |
|---|---|---|---|
|  |  |  |  |

| Crew ||
|---|---|
| Visual Observer | Operator |
|  |  |
| Flight Mission | Notes |

# Drone Flight Log Book

Date:

Drone Model Name

| Location (from - to) | Time |
|---|---|
|  |  |
| Minutes of flight | Battery |
|  |  |

| Weather | Temperature | Wind speed | Wind Direction |
|---|---|---|---|
|  |  |  |  |

| Crew ||
|---|---|
| Visiual Observer | Operator |
|  |  |

| Flight Mission | Notes |
|---|---|

# Drone Flight Log Book

Date:

## Drone Model Name

| Location (from-to) | Time |
|---|---|
|  |  |
| Minutes of flight | Battery |
|  |  |

| Weather | Temperature | Wind speed | Wind Direction |
|---|---|---|---|
|  |  |  |  |

| Crew ||
|---|---|
| Visual Observer | Operator |
|  |  |
| Flight Mission | Notes |

# Drone Flight Log Book

Date:

## Drone Model Name

| Location (from - to) | Time |
|---|---|
|  |  |

| Minutes of flight | Battery |
|---|---|
|  |  |

| Weather | Temperature | Wind speed | Wind Direction |
|---|---|---|---|
|  |  |  |  |

| Crew ||
|---|---|
| Visiual Observer | Operator |
|  |  |

| Flight Mission | Notes |
|---|---|

# Drone Flight Log Book

Date:

## Drone Model Name

| Location (from-to) | Time |
|---|---|
|  |  |
| Minutes of flight | Battery |
|  |  |

| Weather | Temperature | Wind speed | Wind Direction |
|---|---|---|---|
|  |  |  |  |

| Crew ||
|---|---|
| Visual Observer | Operator |
|  |  |
| **Flight Mission** | **Notes** |

# Drone Flight Log Book

Date:

## Drone Model Name

| Location (from - to) | Time |
|---|---|
|  |  |

| Minutes of flight | Battery |
|---|---|
|  |  |

| Weather | Temperature | Wind speed | Wind Direction |
|---|---|---|---|
|  |  |  |  |

| Crew ||
|---|---|
| Visiual Observer | Operator |
|  |  |
| Flight Mission | Notes |

# Drone Flight Log Book

Date:

## Drone Model Name

| Location (from-to) | Time |
|---|---|
|  |  |
| Minutes of flight | Battery |
|  |  |

| Weather | Temperature | Wind speed | Wind Direction |
|---|---|---|---|
|  |  |  |  |

| Crew ||
|---|---|
| Visual Observer | Operator |
|  |  |
| Flight Mission | Notes |

# Drone Flight Log Book

Date:

## Drone Model Name

| Location (from - to) | Time |
|---|---|
|  |  |
| Minutes of flight | Battery |
|  |  |

| Weather | Temperature | Wind speed | Wind Direction |
|---|---|---|---|
|  |  |  |  |

| Crew ||
|---|---|
| Visiual Observer | Operator |
|  |  |
| Flight Mission | Notes |

# Drone Flight Log Book

Date:

## Drone Model Name

| Location (from-to) | Time |
|---|---|
|  |  |
| Minutes of flight | Battery |
|  |  |

| Weather | Temperature | Wind speed | Wind Direction |
|---|---|---|---|
|  |  |  |  |

| Crew ||
|---|---|
| Visual Observer | Operator |
|  |  |
| Flight Mission | Notes |

# Drone Flight Log Book

Date:

## Drone Model Name

| Location (from - to) | Time |
|---|---|
|  |  |

| Minutes of flight | Battery |
|---|---|
|  |  |

| Weather | Temperature | Wind speed | Wind Direction |
|---|---|---|---|
|  |  |  |  |

| Crew ||
|---|---|
| Visiual Observer | Operator |
|  |  |
| Flight Mission | Notes |

# Drone Flight Log Book

Date:

## Drone Model Name

| Location (from-to) | Time |
|---|---|
|  |  |
| Minutes of flight | Battery |
|  |  |

| Weather | Temperature | Wind speed | Wind Direction |
|---|---|---|---|
|  |  |  |  |

| Crew ||
|---|---|
| Visual Observer | Operator |
|  |  |

**Flight Mission** — **Notes**

# Drone Flight Log Book

Date:

## Drone Model Name

| Location (from - to) | Time |
|---|---|
|  |  |

| Minutes of flight | Battery |
|---|---|
|  |  |

| Weather | Temperature | Wind speed | Wind Direction |
|---|---|---|---|
|  |  |  |  |

| Crew ||
|---|---|
| Visiual Observer | Operator |
|  |  |

| Flight Mission | Notes |
|---|---|

# Drone Flight Log Book

Date:

## Drone Model Name

| Location (from-to) | Time |
|---|---|
|  |  |

| Minutes of flight | Battery |
|---|---|
|  |  |

| Weather | Temperature | Wind speed | Wind Direction |
|---|---|---|---|
|  |  |  |  |

| Crew ||
|---|---|
| Visual Observer | Operator |
|  |  |

| Flight Mission | Notes |
|---|---|

# Drone Flight Log Book

Date:

## Drone Model Name

| Location (from - to) | Time |
|---|---|
|  |  |
| Minutes of flight | Battery |
|  |  |

| Weather | Temperature | Wind speed | Wind Direction |
|---|---|---|---|
|  |  |  |  |

| Crew ||
|---|---|
| Visiual Observer | Operator |
|  |  |
| Flight Mission | Notes |

# Drone Flight Log Book

Date:

## Drone Model Name

| Location (from-to) | Time |
|---|---|
|  |  |
| **Minutes of flight** | **Battery** |
|  |  |

| Weather | Temperature | Wind speed | Wind Direction |
|---|---|---|---|
|  |  |  |  |

| Crew ||
|---|---|
| Visual Observer | Operator |
|  |  |
| **Flight Mission** | **Notes** |
|  |  |

# Drone Flight Log Book

Date:

## Drone Model Name

| Location (from - to) | Time |
|---|---|
|  |  |
| Minutes of flight | Battery |
|  |  |

| Weather | Temperature | Wind speed | Wind Direction |
|---|---|---|---|
|  |  |  |  |

| Crew ||
|---|---|
| Visiual Observer | Operator |
|  |  |

| Flight Mission | Notes |
|---|---|
|  |  |

# Drone Flight Log Book

Date:

## Drone Model Name

| Location (from-to) | Time |
|---|---|
|  |  |
| Minutes of flight | Battery |
|  |  |

| Weather | Temperature | Wind speed | Wind Direction |
|---|---|---|---|
|  |  |  |  |

| Crew ||
|---|---|
| Visual Observer | Operator |
|  |  |
| Flight Mission | Notes |

www.ingramcontent.com/pod-product-compliance
Lightning Source LLC
Chambersburg PA
CBHW070940080526
44589CB00013B/1594